I0499193

This Awesome Fucking Notebook Belongs to

....

www.ingramcontent.com/pod-product-compliance
Lightning Source LLC
Chambersburg PA
CBHW070428220526
45466CB00004B/1591
* 9 7 8 1 6 7 4 4 6 6 6 0 6 *